Little Skill Seekers

BEGINNING SOUNDS

SCHOLASTIC

New York • Toronto • London • Auckland • Sydney • New Delhi
Mexico City • Hong Kong • Buenos Aires

Cover Design: Tannaz Fassihi
Cover Illustration: Michael Robertson
Interior Design: Mina Chen
Interior Illustration: Doug Jones

ISBN: 978-1-338-25556-0
Copyright © Scholastic Inc. All rights reserved. Printed in the U.S.A.
First printing, June 2018.

3 4 5 6 7 8 9 10   40   24 23 22 21

Dear Parent,

Welcome to *Little Skill Seekers: Beginning Sounds*! Alphabet recognition and letter-sound relationships are the basis of early reading success—this workbook will help your child develop these skills.

Help your little skill seeker build a strong foundation for learning by choosing more books in the Little Skill Seekers series. The exciting and colorful workbooks in the series are designed to set your child on the path to success. Each book targets essential skills important to your child's development.

Here are some key features of *Little Skill Seekers: Beginning Sounds* and the other workbooks in this series:

- Filled with colorful illustrations that make learning fun and playful

- Provides plenty of opportunity to practice essential skills

- Builds independence as children work through the pages on their own, at their own pace

- Comes in a perfect size that fits easily in a backpack for practice on the go

Now let's get started on this journey to help your child become a successful, lifelong learner!

—The Editors

A is for apple.

Circle the pictures that begin with A.

B is for book.

Circle the pictures that begin with B.

C is for cake.

Circle the pictures that begin with C.

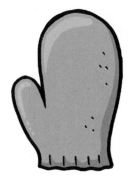

D is for dog.

Circle the pictures that begin with D.

E is for eagle.

Circle the pictures that begin with E.

F is for frog.

Circle the pictures that begin with F.

What sound does each letter make?
Circle the pictures that begin with that sound.

Match each picture to its beginning sound.

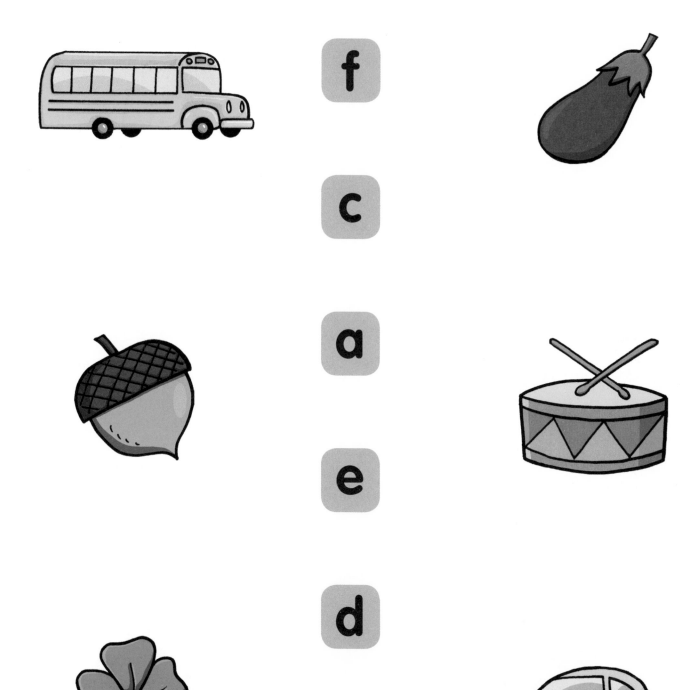

f

c

a

e

d

b

Name each picture.
Circle the letter that makes the beginning sound.

d   f   e

a   b   d

a   d   c

d   f   c

c   a   e

e   d   a

Write the first letter for each word.

c   d   b   e   f   a

_____ irplane

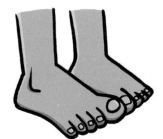

_____ eet

_____ up

_____ ib

_____ gg

_____ oor

G is for goat.

Circle the pictures that begin with G.

14

H is for house.

Circle the pictures that begin with **H**.

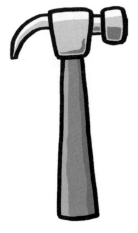

 **I** is for island.

Circle the pictures that begin with I.

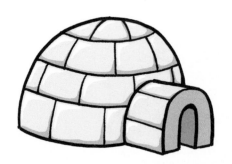

J is for jacket.

Circle the pictures that begin with J.

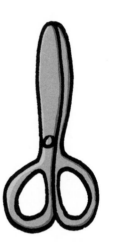

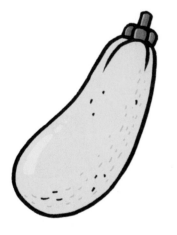

APPLE

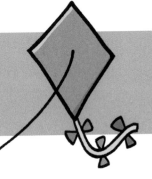

K is for kite.

Circle the pictures that begin with K.

18

 **L** is for lion.

Circle the pictures that begin with L.

What sound does each letter make?
Circle the pictures that begin with that sound.

j

k

i

g

l

h

Draw a line from each picture to its beginning sound.

i

j

g

k

h

l

Name each picture.
Circle the letter that makes the beginning sound.

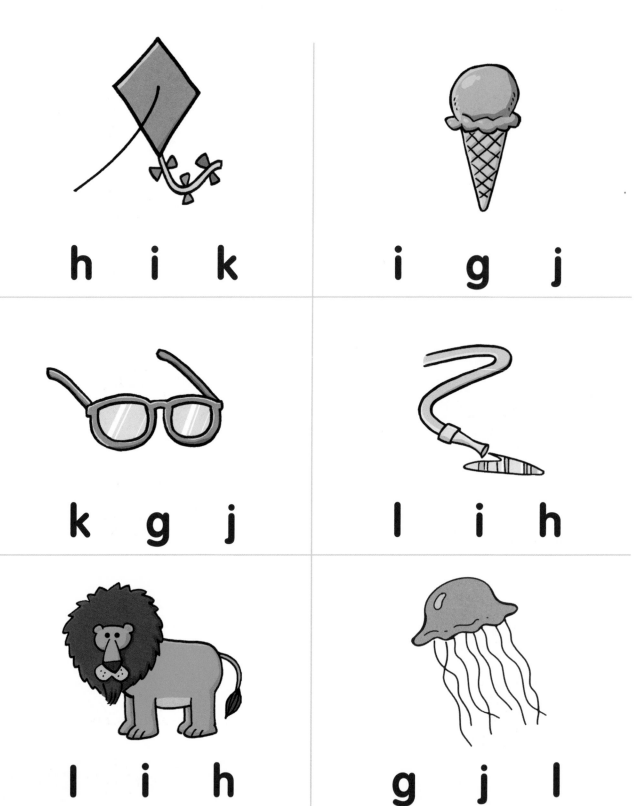

h   i   k

i   g   j

k   g   j

l   i   h

l   i   h

g   j   l

Write the first letter for each word.

k   h   i   l   j   g

____ ron

____ ug

____ eaf

____ lue

____ ing

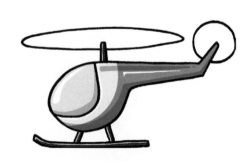

____ elicopter

 **M** is for mirror.

Circle the pictures that begin with **M**.

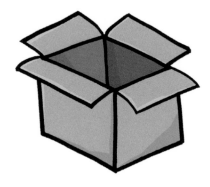

N is for newt.

Circle the pictures that begin with N.

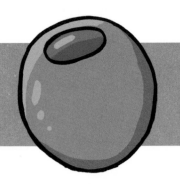

O is for olive.

Circle the pictures that begin with O.

P is for panda.

Circle the pictures that begin with P.

Q is for quail.

Circle the pictures that begin with Q.

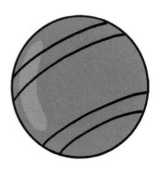

R is for racket.

Circle the pictures that begin with R.

What sound does each letter make?
Circle the pictures that begin with that sound.

p			
o			
r			
q			
n			
m			

Draw a line from each picture to its beginning sound.

o

p

m

q

n

r

Name each picture.
Circle the letter that makes the beginning sound.

m   q   o

p   r   n

m   n   p

o   r   q

r   p   o

n   m   r

Write the first letter for each word.

n   q   m   o   r   p

_____ wl

_____ ueen

_____ ose

_____ ilk

_____ ear

_____ ope

S is for snake.

Circle the pictures that begin with S.

T is for tiger.

Circle the pictures that begin with T.

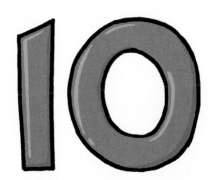

U is for umbrella.

Circle the pictures that begin with U.

V is for vulture.

Circle the pictures that begin with V.

W is for whale.

Circle the pictures that begin with W.

X is for x-ray.

Circle the pictures that begin with X.

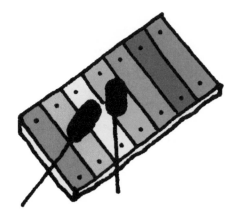

 **Y** is for yarn.

Circle the pictures that begin with Y.

Z is for zebra.

Circle the pictures that begin with Z.

01 2 3

ZOO

What sound does each letter make?
Circle the pictures that begin with that sound.

v

s

z

t

u

y

w

Draw a line from each picture to its beginning sound.

 u

 t

 w

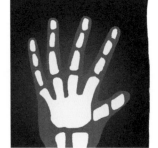

s

z

x

 y

 v

Name each picture.
Circle the letter that makes the beginning sound.

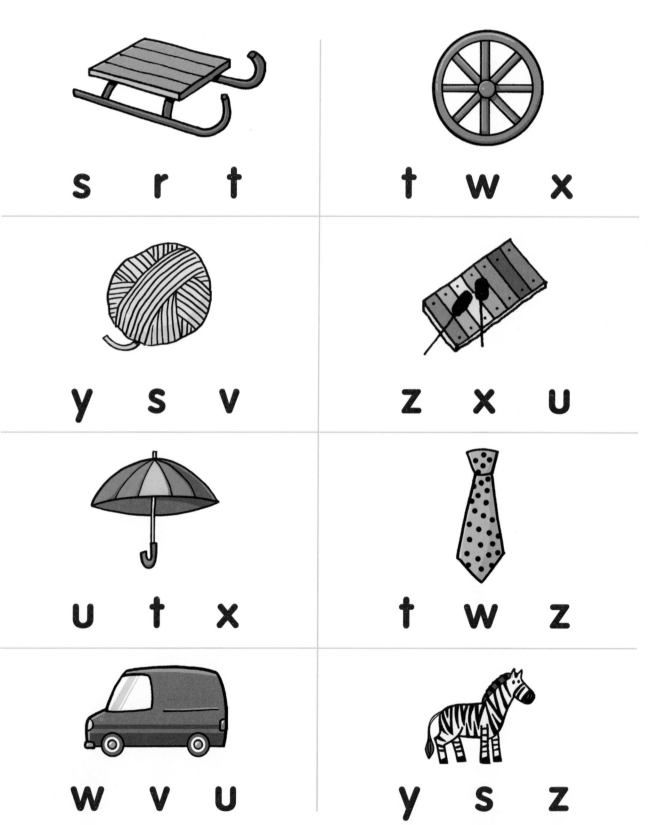

s   r   t

t   w   x

y   s   v

z   x   u

u   t   x

t   w   z

w   v   u

y   s   z

Write the first letter for each word.

t   v   u   x   z   y   w   s

_____ -ray

_____ eb

_____ nicorn

_____ kunk

_____ ak

_____ oo

_____ est

_____ urtle

Name each picture.
Write the first letter in each picture's name.

____

____

____

____

____

____

____

____

____

Name each picture.
Write the first letter in each picture's name.

_____

_____

_____

_____

_____

_____

_____

_____

_____

Name each picture.
Write the first letter in each picture's name.